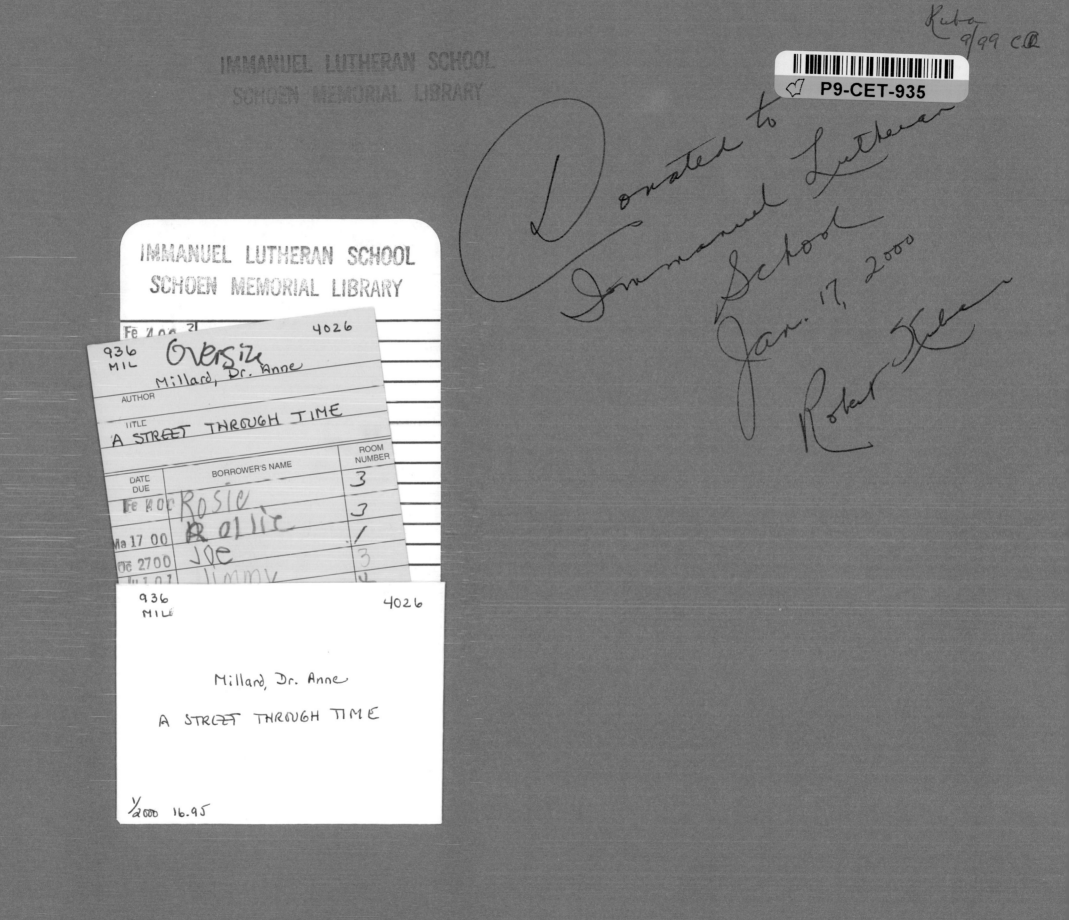

A STREET THROUGH TIME

WRITTEN BY DR. ANNE MILLARD

ILLUSTRATED BY STEVE NOON

DK PUBLISHING, INC.

CONTENTS

A DK Publishing Book
Project Editor Shaila Awan
Art Editor Diane Thistlethwaite
Deputy Managing Editor Dawn Sirett
Managing Art Editors Peter Bailey
and C. David Gillingwater
US Editor William Lach
Production Ruth Cobb
Jacket Design Dean Price
First American Edition, 1998
4 6 8 10 9 7 5 3
Published in the United States by DK Publishing, Inc.
95 Madison Avenue, New York, New York 10016
Visit us on the World Wide Web at http://www.dk.com
Copyright © 1998 Dorling Kindersley Limited, London

Library of Congress Cataloging-in-Publication Data
Millard, Anne.
A street through time/Anne Millard; illustrated by Steve Noon.
p. cm.
Summary: Traces the development of one street from the Stone Age to the present
day, from dirt track to the rebuilding of inns as wine bars, showing how people lived and
what they did all day.
ISBN 0-7894-3426-1
1. Archaeology, Urban–Europe–Juvenile literature. 2. Cities and towns–Europe–
History–Juvenile literature. 3. City and town life–Europe–History–Juvenile literature.
(1. Cities and towns–History. 2. City and town life –History.)
I. Noon, Steve, ill. II. Title.
CC171.M55 1998
936–dc21
98-3226
CIP
AC

Color reproduction by Dot Gradations, UK.
Printed and bound in Singapore by Tien Wah Press.

THE STORY OF A STREET

SOME STREETS AND EVEN SOME WHOLE TOWNS ARE VERY NEW. BUT THERE ARE SOME TOWNS AND STREETS THAT ARE VERY old. Come with us and explore an old, old street. You will see how it has changed from a camp of nomadic hunter-gatherers, into a settled village, then a town, and then a city. Its progress has by no means been smooth! Sometimes the people living there have enjoyed peace and prosperity. At other times they have faced war, sickness, and poverty. Some buildings in the street have survived, while others have been rebuilt many, many times. You'll find out too, how people's way of life and standard of living have changed – not always for the better!

THE STREET'S INHABITANTS

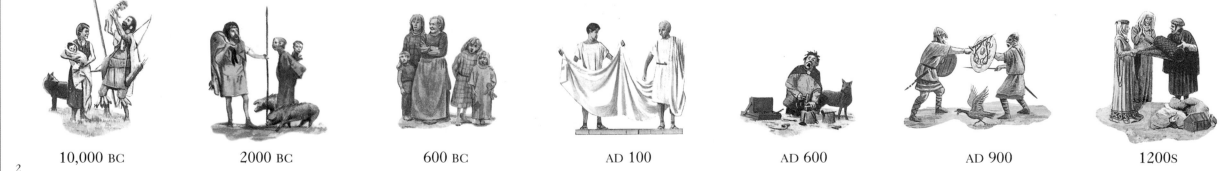

10,000 BC   2000 BC   600 BC   AD 100   AD 600   AD 900   1200s

A Riverside Settlement

The river is central to the story of the street. Some 12,000 years ago it drew wandering Stone Age hunters, seeking water and another source of food. About 4,000 years ago, farming had replaced hunting as a way of life and people settled by its banks. It was a good supply of water for people, animals, and crops. Later the river brought trade to the new village, helping it to grow and prosper, but it sometimes brought troubles, too, such as invaders and disease. You can trace the changing role of the river from age to age as the story of the street unfolds.

Changing Times

For hundreds of years people farmed and lived in the village by the river. They slowly began to cut down the trees that covered the land, using them for fuel, to make tools and weapons, and as building materials. The farmers' lives changed only slowly until the arrival of the Romans caused a total upheaval! By about AD 100 the village had become a town with all the benefits of Rome's comfortable way of life. The local people lived in small apartments and traditional huts, while the Romans occupied villas and large houses. Everything changed again when Rome's Empire was invaded by barbarians. The town was destroyed, our street became part of a small village, and people's standard of living plummeted. The struggle to survive and prosper began anew. But it was to be shattered again, this time by Vikings in AD 900.

From Village to City

Eventually powerful kings and lords put an end to the Viking threat. Traders who now sailed up the river helped the village grow into a town. By the late 1600s the town had survived plagues and wars, though the castle was reduced to ruins. But the real changes came in the late 1700s and early 1800s. Improvements in farming methods meant more people could be fed by fewer farmers on less land. New machines brought the Industrial Revolution to the street, which was now in a rapidly growing city. There were new industries, new methods of transportation, and new wealth. But for some life became even harder.

The Street Today

Our street remains in a city that has survived wars and spread so far that all the old forests and farmland have disappeared. The pace of change has become so rapid that people who lived in our street only 150 years ago would not recognize the modern businesses along the riverbank. Generally, people are much better off now than their ancestors were. But what will happen over the next 12,000 years?

The Time Traveler

This is Henry Hyde. He is hidden in the pictures of each historical period. Henry works in a museum in the present day, but he has a secret: he has a time machine. He can travel back to the past and see how people lived and how the objects in his museum were used.

| 1400s | 1500s | 1600s | 1700s | Early 1800s | Late 1800s | Today |

Forest stretches across the land and there are very few people. The next tribe is 50 miles away.

The forest is full of animals and the hunters have had success.

STONE AGE HUNTERS (10,000 BC)

Once upon a time, everyone lived by hunting, fishing, and gathering food. People were nomads, moving across the land in small groups seeking food and temporary shelter. This tribe has just found a place to spend the winter. The camp is the start of our street.

Can you spot the woman using a leather bag to carry water?

Find the old woman telling children stories about the tribe.

Deer skull – symbol of the woodland god

Chopping wood

Gathering berries

Priest

Preparing animal hides

Storyteller

Fishing

4

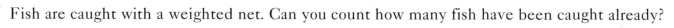

The animals' meat is eaten, their fur and hides make clothes and tents, and their bones make tools. 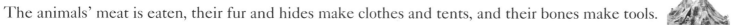 Some of the meat is dried and stored, ready for the winter months.

The canoes are made of logs.

Dogs are the only animals people have tamed. Find the dogs fighting over food scraps.

Animal hide tent

Cutting meat

Making a fire

Plucking a duck

Flint worker

Hunters

Making a canoe

5

Tools and weapons are made of flint. This flint worker has found a good source nearby. The tribe's priest is calling on the spirit of the forest to bless the new camp.

FIRST FARMERS (2000 BC)

More than eight thousand years have passed and people have learned how to grow crops and keep animals. They have also developed new skills, such as pottery making, cloth weaving, and metalworking. The site by the river now has a permanent settlement with huts.

Stone circle

Using a bow and arrow

Thatched wooden hut

Hunter

Palisade

Pottery kiln

Wolf.

Threshing

Winnowing

Spinning Weaving Sewing

Harpooning fish

6

Find the barrow (mound), where the dead are buried.

Can you spot the man who has just returned from hunting a deer?

Wheat and barley grow in the fields. The crops are cut with a sickle made from a sharp piece of flint. The people believe that this goddess makes their crops grow.

Barrow

Cutting crops

Cutting firewood

Roasting meat

Grinding wheat

Making a basket

Blacksmith

Metal mold

Making flint tools

Find an old man teaching his grandson how to use a bow and arrow.

Spot the blacksmith busy making bronze tools.

7

Several villages have joined together to build a stone circle to honor the gods. Fire is a great danger in wooden huts with thatched roofs. It can spread quickly.

The chief has built a stronghold, called a fort, on the hill. It is made of wood.

The chief and his warriors, who live in the fort, celebrate a battle victory.

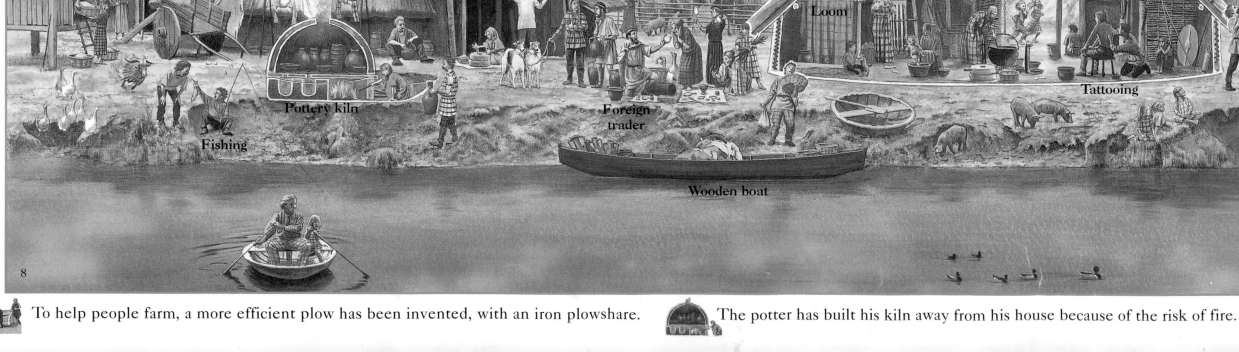

THE IRON AGE (600 BC)

Hundreds of years pass. People have now found out how to smelt iron to make better tools and weapons. The village has prospered, but there are battles with neighboring tribes, who are fierce rivals.

The men are proud and quick-tempered. Spot a fight brewing.

Can you find the dog that is being chased by a goose?

Ancient stone circle

Sacred grove

Enemy heads

Cattle

Rival warriors

Food hut

Thatched wooden hut

Palisade

Loom

Tattooing

Pottery kiln

Foreign trader

Fishing

Wooden boat

8

To help people farm, a more efficient plow has been invented, with an iron plowshare.

The potter has built his kiln away from his house because of the risk of fire.

Priests offer captured enemy weapons to the gods by throwing them into the river.

After the warriors and the priests, the blacksmith is the most important man.

Can you find three wooden statues set up to honor the gods?

Spot two monuments in the hills from earlier times.

Fort

Ancient barrow

Guard

Chief

Thatchers

Plowing

Priests

Prisoners

Blacksmith

Carpenter

Coracle (boat)

9

ROMAN TIMES (AD 100)

The Roman Empire has spread across much of Europe, bringing a new way of life. Our village has become a town with hundreds of people. The town has large stone buildings, and a bridge has been built across the river for the first time.

Spot the very rare and expensive pet (a cat).

Children from rich families attend school. Can you find the schoolroom?

Statue of Jupiter

Temple

Ancient stone circle

Small apartment

Carpenters

Wall paintings

School

Domus

Bedroom

Bedroom

Barber's shop

Pottery shop

Baker's shop

Tavern

Toilet

Atrium

Kitchen

Stove

Slaves

Local hunter

Wooden bridge

A rich family lives in a townhouse, or a domus. The domus has beautiful statues and paintings. In the amphitheater, crowds often come to see gladiators fight to the death.

Native huts

Fort

Amphitheater

Roman soldiers

Basilica

Bathhouse

Wine warehouse

Crane

Fountain

Pulse

Brick building

Merchant ship

Imported wine in amphorae (jars)

Most hard work is done by slaves. Find a group of slaves arriving.

Find the local chief visiting a Roman official.

The fort is where Roman soldiers are stationed. They drill and march, so they are always ready for action. Ships bring goods such as wine from all over the Empire.

THE INVADERS (AD 600)

Barbarians have swept across Europe, destroying the Roman way of life. A group have settled in the ruins of our town. All the Roman comforts, such as baths and piped water, have been forgotten.

Can you spot the ruins of three important Roman buildings near the settlement?

Find a woman weaving inside a hut.

Ancient stone circle

Columns from Roman temple

Wolves

Shepherd boy

Sheep pen

Thatched wooden hut

Chief

Weaving

Laying fish traps

Wooden boat

12

The simple huts are made of wood. The chief has the biggest hut.  Wood is used for cooking, heating, and building. Find five people chopping or gathering wood.

Roman fort

Ancient barrow

Roman amphitheater

Chief's hut

Food stores

Dried meat

Beggars

Vegetable patch

Blacksmith

Carpenter

Slave woman

Washing clothes

Console

Wolves have taken a sheep. The shepherd boy tries to drive them away with his sling. Who has found a Roman statue?

Sticks are used to make wooden fences. This stops the sheep from straying. Pigs roam through the village, scavenging. This one takes a bite out of the laundry!

VIKING RAIDERS (AD 900)

The barbarians have now been settled for hundreds of years. They have become Christians and have grown prosperous. They have a king who gives his orders through the local chiefs. Now a new danger has appeared – fierce Viking raiders seeking treasure and slaves.

Ancient stone circle

Stone church

Graveyard

Hole for smoke

Toilet

Viking longship

Viking

14

Ancient barrow

Chief's hall with
wooden roof

Thatched
wooden hut

Sail
rolled up

Jetty

MEDIEVAL VILLAGE (1200s)

More than three hundred years have passed. The king has given the land to a lord, who has built a castle to protect the people from Viking raiders. The lord uses mounted warriors, called knights, to race to trouble spots. In return, most people have had to give up much of their freedom.

Villagers use the common land to graze animals. Can you see this pasture?

Find the entertainers in the marketplace.

Common land

Ancient stone circle

Spire

Fallow land (unplanted)

Glass windows (used by the church and rich only)

Church

Peasant's house

Cobbler's shop

Baker's shop

Reed cutter's boat

16

The villagers live in small houses. Their animals are often stabled in part of the house.  Today is market day. Some people have come from other villages to buy and sell goods.

Keep

Stone castle

Castle wall

Windmill on site of ancient barrow

Miller's house

Barley strips growing

Wheat strips growing

Chimney

Knight's stone house

Timber-framed house

Inn

Dentist

Milkmaid

Blacksmith

Peddler

Foreign merchant

Sailboat

The lord's wife is buying cloth from a foreign merchant. Can you see them?

Can you spot the traveling dentist?

A ball game with boys from the neighboring village is turning into a rowdy riot! It is cheaper to bring goods by river and safer, too – there may be outlaws in the forest!

MEDIEVAL TOWN (1400s)

Thanks to the trade brought by boats up the river, the village has grown into a town. Its citizens have purchased a charter from their lord. This allows them to run the town. Some of the merchants have become very rich.

Can you guess what the inn is called, from the sign outside it?

Find the doctor treating his patient by bleeding his arm.

Church

Collecting firewood

Wine merchant's house

Bedroom

Doctor

Shutter

Cobbler's shop

Weaver's shop

Baker's shop

Religious procession

Kitchen

Lending money

Selling wine

Cellar

Stone bridge

18.

This man has found an ancient helmet.

In winter, many people use their right to collect firewood from the forest.

Stone castle

Turret

Miller's house

Windmill

Town guard

Deer hunters

Gibbet

Guildhall

Tapestry

Glass window

Market cross

Inn

Armorer's workshop

Stocks

Black rats come off the ship

Foreign merchant's ship

Lord and his wife return from a visit

19

THE PLAGUE STRIKES! (1500s)

The Black Death arrived in Europe from Asia in 1347, carried by the fleas on black rats. Over the next 300 years it kept returning. Most people who caught the plague died. This disease has now hit our prosperous town.

Plague pit

Church

Merchant's house

Baker's shop

Burglars

Death cart

Kitchen

Printing press

Cellar

Painting a white cross

Soldiers

How many people have died in the streets? Who has just found some? Black spots under the arms were a sign of plague.

A cart collects the dead and takes them to a plague pit, where the bodies are buried together. 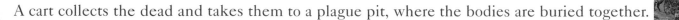 The open sewers in the streets attract the rats. They are everywhere now!

Stone castle

Miller's house

Windmill

Gibbet

Guildhall

Inn

Doctor

Apothecary's shop

Escaping by riverboat

Spot the apothecary mixing a potion to find a cure for the plague. The baker continues working. Can you see him?

A white cross on a door shows there is plague inside. No one can leave the house. The doctor wears a strange mask, hoping this will stop him from catching the infection.

UNDER ATTACK! (1600s)

War has broken out. The people are fighting over religion and about who should rule the country. The castle and town are both under attack, and the townspeople are losing! Not even the castle walls can withstand the pounding of the improved cannons.

Church

Enemy soldiers

Cobbler's shop

Tailor's shop

Kitchen

Merchant's house

Printing press

Town soldiers

Stone castle

Windmill

Miller's house

Doctor

Stone house

Inn

Cannon

How many buildings have been set on fire by cannonballs?

A brave woman has decided to fight back. Can you see her?

23

AN AGE OF ELEGANCE (1700s)

Peace has returned and the town is prospering again. Some houses have been repaired; others have been rebuilt in the latest style. The wealthy citizens have a lot of spare time. They pride themselves on their polite manners, their learning, and their elegant parties.

Spire

Church

Clock

Brick building

Shoe shop

Dress shop

Wig shop

Servants' bedroom

Servants' bedroom

Wife's bedroom

Husband's bedroom

Reading poetry

Playing cards

Dancing

Sitting room

Laundry room

Kitchen

Milkmaid

Can you find the chimney sweeper and his climbing boy? Who has found a treasure chest that was buried during the war?

24

Squire's house

Castle ruins

Lord's mansion

Find the statue of the previous lord, who defended the town.

Find the rat catcher. No wonder the plague has died out!

Inn

Guest room

Highwayman

Town hall

Guest room

Hat shop

Statue

Stagecoach

Bar

Mail coach

Sedan chair

Rat catcher

Coffee shop

Chimney sweeper

Sailboat

25

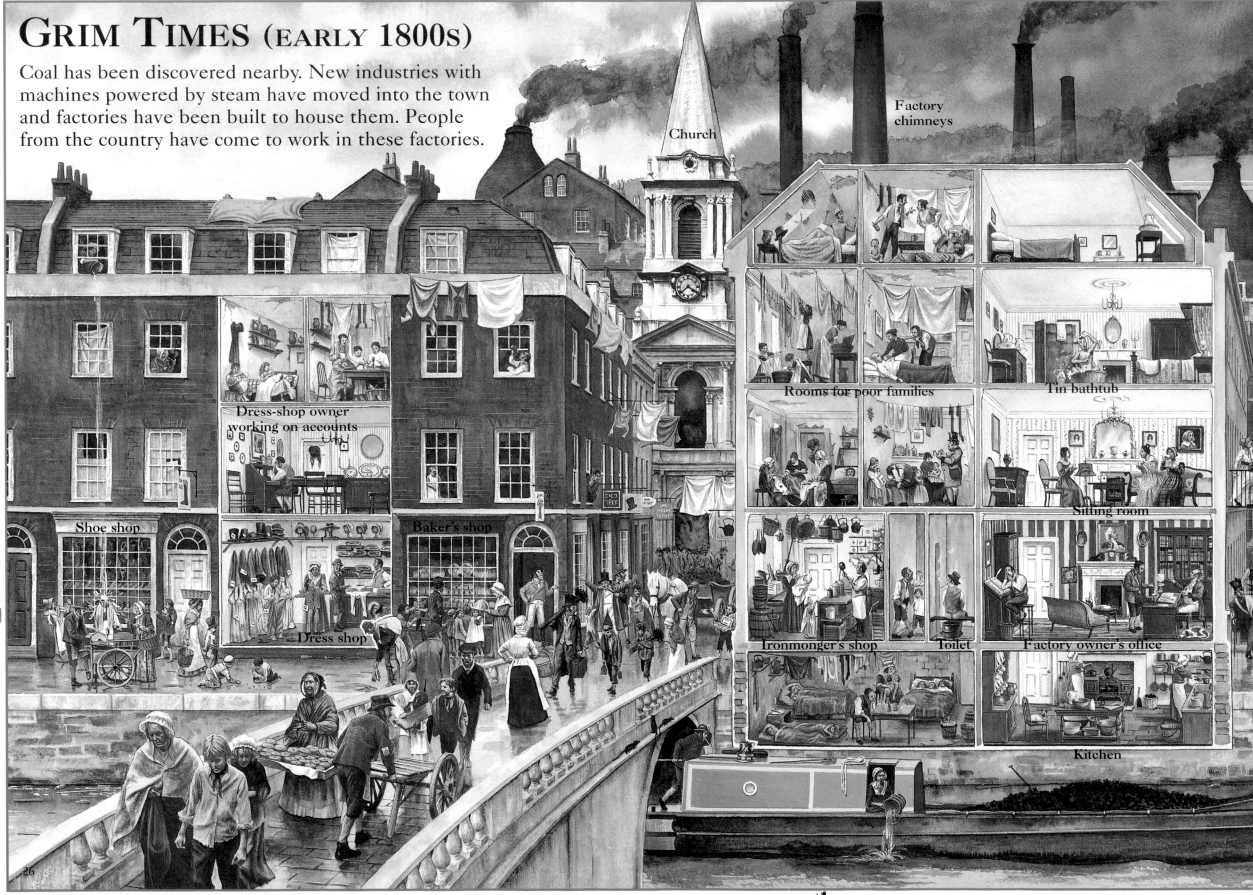

GRIM TIMES (EARLY 1800s)

Coal has been discovered nearby. New industries with machines powered by steam have moved into the town and factories have been built to house them. People from the country have come to work in these factories.

Church

Factory chimneys

Dress-shop owner working on accounts

Rooms for poor families

Tin bathtub

Shoe shop

Baker's shop

Sitting room

Dress shop

Ironmonger's shop

Toilet

Factory owner's office

Kitchen

Most houses are crowded. Can you find the house in which only one family lives?

Find the man whose roof is leaking.

26

Heavy goods such as coal are carried by barges. The barges are pulled along by horses on the riverbank. These men are using children to pick pockets for them.

Poor children have to work too, so that they can earn money. Most cannot read or write.

There are no homes to care for orphans. Some live and sleep in the street.

A few brave men are experimenting with a new form of travel. What is it? Who cannot sleep because of noisy neighbors?

Hot-air balloon

Castle ruins

Coal mines

Pottery kiln

Town hall

Gambling

Pickpockets

Inn

Pawnbroker's shop

Liquor store

Milk cart

Orphans

Coal barge

27

With the overcrowded houses, dirt, and polluted water, many people get sick.

Some people drink to forget their misery. This drunk is in danger of falling off the roof!

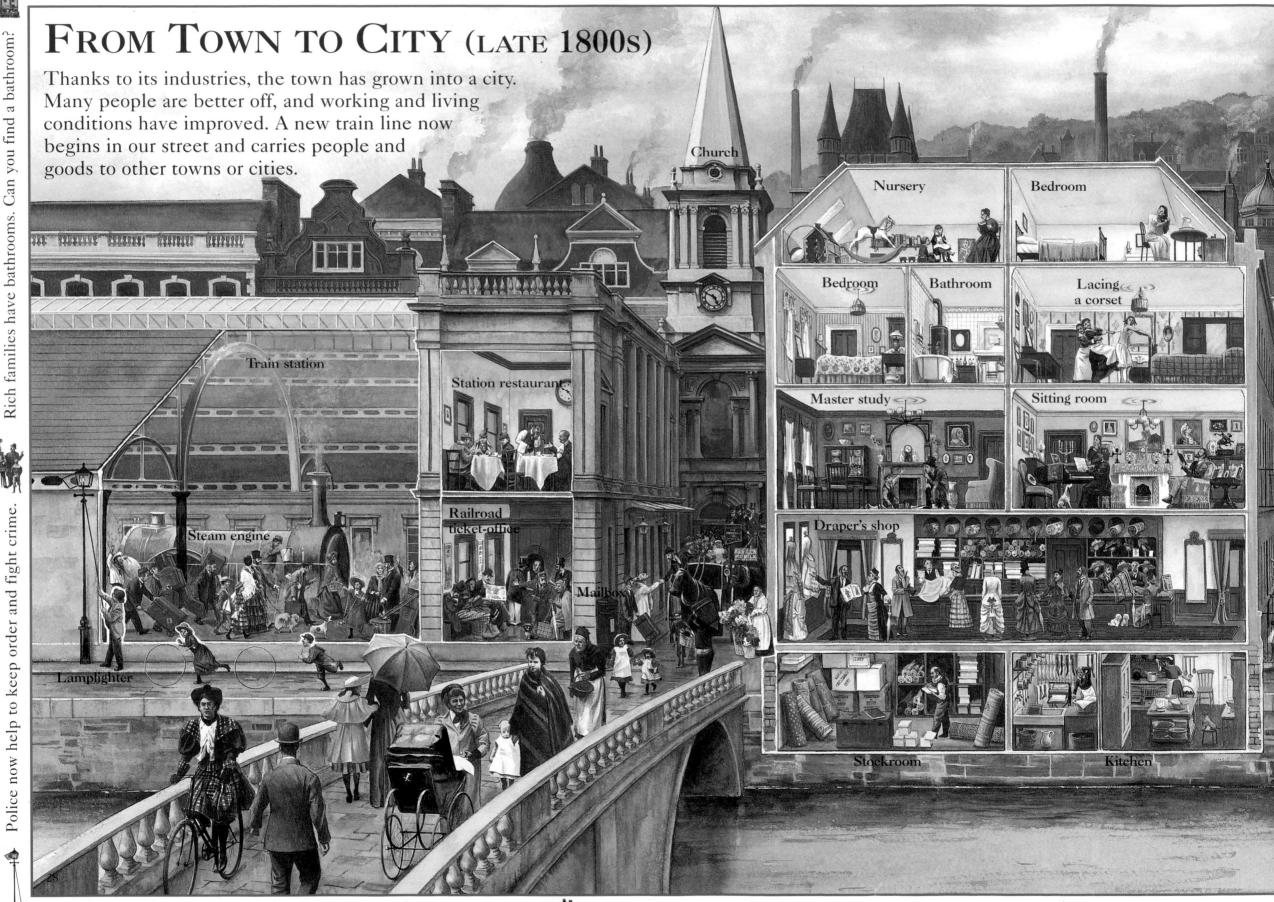

FROM TOWN TO CITY (LATE 1800s)

Thanks to its industries, the town has grown into a city. Many people are better off, and working and living conditions have improved. A new train line now begins in our street and carries people and goods to other towns or cities.

Church

Nursery

Bedroom

Bedroom

Bathroom

Lacing a corset

Train station

Station restaurant

Master study

Sitting room

Steam engine

Railroad ticket-office

Draper's shop

Mailbox

Lamplighter

Stockroom

Kitchen

Rich families have bathrooms. Can you find a bathroom?

Police now help to keep order and fight crime.

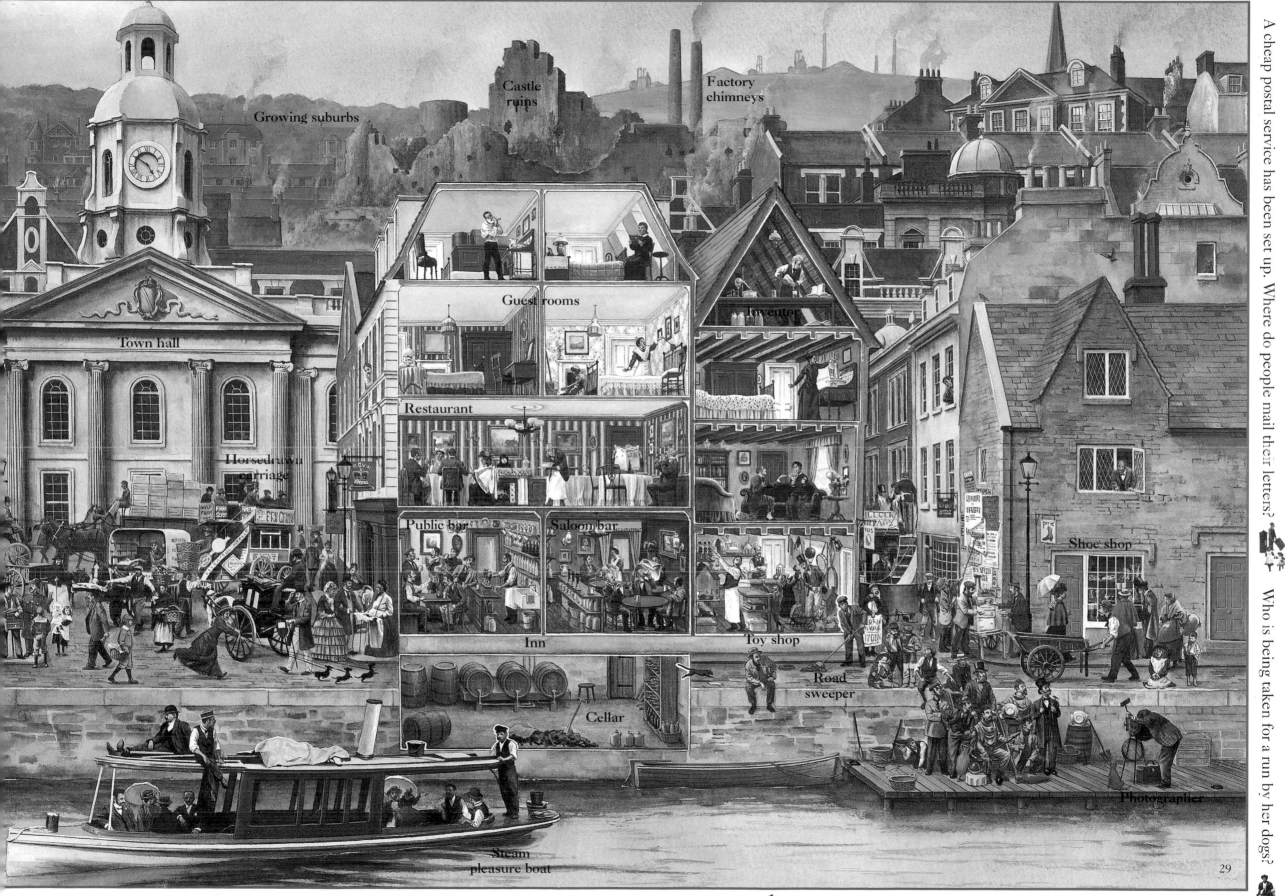

For the first time, people can travel to other cities quickly and cheaply by using the trains.

Steam engines are now used to power boats as well as locomotives.

A cheap postal service has been set up. Where do people mail their letters?

Who is being taken for a run by her dogs?

Growing suburbs

Castle ruins

Factory chimneys

Town hall

Guest rooms

Inventor

Restaurant

Shoe shop

Horsedrawn carriage

Public bar

Saloon bar

Inn

Toy shop

Road sweeper

Cellar

Photographer

Steam pleasure boat

29

The photographer is about to take a picture of the men who are going to try out their new diving suits.

Although it was not common, some daring women rode bicycles.

THE STREET TODAY

In recent years there has been much change in our city. Modern businesses have replaced most heavy industries, the town has become more environmentally aware, and leisure time has increased for most people.

Crane

Office block

Apartments

Hair salon

Artist's studio

Church

Dentist

Bathroom

Lawyer's office

Café

Museum

Bookshop

Bank's office

Museum shop

Clothes shop

Bank

Safe

Gymnasium

Jogger

Rowboat

Spot new forms of communication, such as a TV or phone.

Men dredging the river have found a chest. Who dropped it and when?

Many people who work in the city live in houses or apartments that have recently been built. The river is used for leisure activities, such as rowing.

Castle ruins

Tourists

Town hall

Nursery　Bathroom

Sitting room　Kitchen

Café

Wine bar　Antique shop

Streetcar

Shoe shop

Restaurant

Motorboat

Dredger

Canoe

Why is the bank manager in for a nasty shock? A crane is being used to construct a highrise. Can you see the crane?

31

TIME-TRAVELING QUIZ

Below is a list of some of the things Henry Hyde has seen while visiting all the periods in our street's history. Can you find these things too?

STONE AGE HUNTERS

The hunters start a fire for cooking by rubbing two wooden sticks together. Find the man using this method.

FIRST FARMERS

Reeds growing near the settlement are used to make baskets. Can you find the woman weaving a basket?

THE IRON AGE

Can you see the warrior being tattooed? Vegetable dye is used to paint the patterns on his body.

ROMAN TIMES

A crane is used to lift heavy building material. It is worked by slaves. Can you find the crane in the street?

THE INVADERS

Find two different wooden boats used by barbarian tribes.

VIKING RAIDERS

The local people are now all Christians. Find the graveyard where they bury their dead.

MEDIEVAL VILLAGE

Important buildings are now made of stone. Can you find three stone buildings?

MEDIEVAL TOWN

What structure has been built in stone across the river?

THE PLAGUE STRIKES!

With a printing press, a book only takes a few days to print. Find the press that has been abandoned during the plague.

UNDER ATTACK!

Garbage and sewage is still dumped in the street. Spot two places where it is trickling into the river.

AN AGE OF ELEGANCE

Can you find the highwayman examining his loot from a recent raid?

GRIM TIMES

Two children are playing a game of marbles in the street. Can you see them?

FROM TOWN TO CITY

There is now a new toy shop in the street. A boy is busy choosing a toy soldier to buy. Can you find the shop?

THE STREET TODAY

How many of the objects in the museum can you find in earlier periods in the book?

GLOSSARY

Amphitheater (page 11*): An oval or round building with seats, used by Romans for animal shows and gladiator fights.

Amphorae (page 11): Clay jars with two handles, used by Romans to keep wine and other liquids.

Apothecary (page 21): A person who makes and sells medicine.

Atrium (page 10): A central hall in a Roman house with the rooms opening off it.

Barbarians (page 3): Romans referred to people who lived outside the Roman Empire as "barbarians." In particular, the word is often applied to people from north and northeastern Europe who began invading the Empire after AD 200.

Barrow (page 7): An old form of grave, consisting of an earth mound over burial chambers.

Basilica (page 11): A Roman building where legal rights and town functions were held.

BC and AD (page 2): BC means years *before* the birth of Christ. AD refers to the years *after* the birth of Christ.

Charter (page 18): A written document given by a king or a lord granting rights to someone.

Coracle (page 9): A small oval boat made of woven sticks and covered by a waterproof material.

Domus (page 10): A Roman townhouse used by a wealthy family.

Gibbet (page 19): A wooden gallows where dangerous criminals were put to death by hanging.

Guilds (page 19): Unions of craftsmen or merchants that controlled working standards, conditions, and prices. They also cared for members in trouble.

Guildhall (page 19): A place where guild members met to run their guilds and the town.

Industrial Revolution (page 3): A period during the 1700s and 1800s when there were huge changes in the way people lived and worked. This was brought about by inventions that led to factories producing goods faster than people could at home.

Iron Age (page 8): Although people were experimenting with iron by 1100 BC, the period of history known as the Iron Age began about 900 BC, when iron replaced bronze to make tools and weapons.

Jetty (page 15): A landing place on a river or in a harbor.

Keep (page 17): The strongest part of a castle was the stone building, known as the keep.

Nomads (page 4): People who wander from place to place seeking food and shelter.

Palisade (page 6): A fence of strong wooden poles built around a fort or village to help defend it from enemies and wild animals.

Roman Empire (page 3): About 200 BC Rome began conquering other lands and created an empire that was to last in western Europe until AD 476. At its height, it covered much of Europe, North Africa, and parts of the Middle East.

Sling (page 13): A piece of leather or woven material used to hurl stones.

Stocks (page 19): A wooden frame with holes for feet, neck, and hands – used to punish smalltime crooks.

Stone Age (page 3): A period of history when tools and weapons were made mostly of stone. It began when the earliest people made their first tools and ended when metal was introduced.

Sulfur (page 20): A yellow mineral that burns with choking smoke and a horrible smell.

Threshing (page 6): Beating grain with flails (special sticks) to get the grain out of the ears.

Winnowing (page 6): Tossing grains into the air to separate them from their light cases.

Vikings (page 3): Fierce warriors from Norway, Sweden, and Denmark. They raided and settled in parts of Europe between AD 700 and 1100.

*Note: The page numbers refer to the first page on which the word appears.